Excel: Quick Start Guide - Mastering Excel (Excel, Microsoft Office, Functions and Formulas, Macros, MS Excel 2016, Shortcuts,)

By:

Rick Loftus

Published by 42 Enterprises Publishing,
All Rights Reserved,
Copyright 2016, Cincinnati, Ohio

Table of Contents

Introduction 3

Chapter 1: Excel Basics 4

Chapter 2: Excel Functions 9

Chapter 3: Excel Formulas 14

Chapter 4: Data Analysis 17

Chapter 5: Macros 20

Chapter 6: Ms Excel 2016 24

Chapter 7: Excel Shortcuts 28

Conclusion 32

Introduction

There is a lot that canbe done ona computer today whether in a work situation or just at home. Computers are slowly becoming an important accessory at home and in offices and this ismainly because of data storage. A computer can take in so much data, and the data can bekept safe for a very long time.

Excel is one of the best spreadsheet programs youwill get today,which can help you in the storage of data. This is not just what the program is good at; it can help you organize your data for easier retrieval and at the same time help you analyze the same data with ease, using its inbuilt tools.

Sometimes back, only a few people were using Excel, because it was used to analyze the most complicated data but today, a lot of people have seen the need to learn Excel in order totake advantage of its amazing features tomake their work much easier.

Today, use of Excel is seen in so many areas, for instance in the creation of budgets, in the creation of invoices, in theorganizing of training logs among so many other areas. This is because Excel is able to handle different types of data better than any other program out there.

For this reason, Excel skills are very important for anyone that wants to work better and to grab better job opportunities out there. This eBook has providedall the basics you need tomaster in order to get started in Excel at the best footing.

Chapter 1:
Excel Basics

Microsoft Excel is one of the most used applications in the world today. So many people, individuals as well as business people use Microsoft Excel every day. This is a program that can be used to do a lot of things for instance to enter all kinds of data in a computer, to perform statistical, financial and mathematical calculations among other important functions. Microsoft Excel is very important in the day to day working of people in offices as they need to enter data on an everyday basis as well as manipulate data that has already been stored in their databases. This means that this is one of the most important software applications you need to master today.

There is a lot about Microsoft Excel that you need to learn about in order to get started with use of excel in the right way:

Ribbon

When you open Excel, it selects the ribbons Home tab. You have to learn how to customize and to minimize the ribbon. On the ribbon, you will get Tabs like File, Home, Insert, Page Layout, Formulas, Data, Review and View. Most of the commands you will be using in Excel will be found in the Home Tab. Minimizing the ribbonwill give you the extra space you need on the screen to work better. You can achieve thisthrough clicking anywhere on the ribbon,then clicking on the Minimize the Ribbon button. Customizing the ribbon on theother hand helps you to create your own Tab and add some of the commands you feel will be useful to you as you work with Excel. Do this by clicking anywhere on the ribbon, then clicking on the Customize the Ribbon Button. Select the new

Tab option and then add thecommands you like. You can rename your new tab to make it more personal.

Workbook

A workbook is the name used to refer to your Excel file. When you open Excel, a blank workbook opens automatically. If you have already created a workbook, you can access it through the File command on your Excel tab. To create a new workbook, click on New and then select Create. This can be done if you want to start all over again, and not rely on the workbook that pops up automatically when you open Excel.

Worksheets

A worksheet refers to the collection of cells where you will enter your data for later use. By default, your Excel workbook will contain three worksheets, which are named sheet1, sheet2 and sheet3 by default. When you open the program, it will select the first worksheet for you. Its name will be seen on the sheet tab, which is at the bottom of the document. You can give your sheets a more specific name though, by clicking on the sheet tab of the sheet you want torename, then selecting Rename.

You are allowed to add as many worksheets as you want on yourworkbook and this can be done pretty fast. Click on the insert Worksheet tab that is at the bottom of the document window and one sheet will be added on your workbook.

You can change the location of a worksheet as well, by clicking on the worksheet that you want to move and dragging it to the location here you want it to be.

To get rid of a worksheet, click on it and then select delete.

Worksheets can be copied and paste in a new location too, especially if they have information that is needed in another workbook.

Formatting cells

This is done when you want to change the appearance of a number without necessarily changingthe number itself. To do this, right click on the cell where the number you want toformat is, and thenclick Format Cells. Youwill be given a preview of how thenumber will looklike before youfinish formatting. Again onthis, youcan change the cell color and add borders to change its appearance to yourliking.

Excel special features

Excel has some special features that will make your work much easier when you are trying to achieve something for instance the Find and Replace features, which can help you to quickly find a certain text and replace it with other text. To find a certain text, go to the Home Tab then click on Find and Select. You can now type the text that you want to find. There is the Go To special feature too which can help you to quickly select all the cells with comments, formulas, constants, conditional formatting, and data validation among others.

Excel templates

These are used to create a workbook in instances when you do not want to create one from scratch. There are so many free templates that are available for Excel users, which you can use every time you want to come up with a workbook. To do this, click on the File Tab, then select New the Sample Templates and you will have a variety of templates to choose from.

Keyboard shortcuts

In order to work faster, you might need to learn a few keyboard shortcuts which allow you to work with your keyboard instead of your mouse. If you want to select an entire range, press CTRL+a. If youpress CTRL +a again, youwill select the entire sheet. To copy a range, use CTLR+c, and to cut therange, press CTRL+x. us CTRL+v in order to pastethe range youhave copied or cut in another location. To undo allthis operation, press CTRL+z. use CTRL together with the arrow keys in order to move from one end of therange to the other. There are so many shortcuts that can make your working with Excel much easier. They will be discussed later on in this book.

Sharing excel data

It is important to learn how to share excel data with Word documents and other files. You can do this by use of copy + paste options. You can also include the link of the source of data in Excel with the destination data in a Word documents. This ensures that any changes you will make in the Excel data is automatically updated in the word document as well.

Protecting Excel data

It is important to protect any data that you save in a computer. With Excel data, you can encrypt your Excel files with passwords so that you will be the only one with access to them.

To do this, select File Tab on your workbook, then click on Save As. Go to the Tools button and click on General Options. Enter your password and then click on OK. You will be asked to reenter your password just to be sure that you can clearly remember it. Now enter the file name and click on Save.

Chapter 2:
Excel Functions

Every function in Excel has the same structure. An example of afunction is: SUM (A1:A4), where the name of the function here is SUM. Inside the brackets you will get the arguments. This function basically means that you need to add something to cells A1, A2, A3 and A4. Since it is not always easy to remember the function and arguments to use in every task you will be working on, Excel provides an Insert Function feature, which will help you so much with this.

To insert a function, select the cell where you want the function inserted, then click on Insert Function button. Look for the function you want to use and click Ok when you find it. Select the range and the criteria and then hit OK.

Functions in Excel are meant to help you save time. Here are some of the functions you need to familiarize yourself with as a beginner:

Count and sum

These are the functions that are used themost in Excel. You can count and sum in Excel based on a certain criteria or anumber of criteria. If for instance you want to count thenumber of cells thathas numbers, you will use the COUNT function. Use the COUNTif function when you want to count the number of cells based on one criteria. Use COUNTifsfunctions to count cells based on a number of criteria.

The Sum function theother hand is used to sum a range of cells. SUMif function will be used to sum cells basedon a single criteria while SUMifs will beused to sum a number ofcells using multiple criteria.

Logical

There are a number of Excels logical functions you need to learn about, which are IF, AND and OR functions.

The IF function will be used to check whether a certain condition has been met or not. The results will be True or False.

The AND Function will return True if all the conditions are true and it will return False if all the conditions are not true.

The OR Function will return True if any of the conditions are True and it will return false if all the conditions will not be true.

Note that all these Functions can check up to 255 conditions.

Cell References

These are also very important functions to learn in Excel. They include Relative, Absolute and Mixed references.

The Relative reference is the one that has been set by Excel as default. Every cell references its two neighbors on the left.

Time and date

In order to enter a date in Excel, '/' or '-'are the characters which should be used. Inorder to enter time, you use a colon.

A date and time can be entered in time cell. If you want to get the year of a certain date, the YEAR function will be used.

The DATE function accepts only three arguments, which are the year, the monthand the day.

Usethe NOW function in order to get the current date and time accurately. If you usethe today function, youwillonly getthedate of today. There is the HOUR, Min and SEC functions which can be used to return the hours, minutes and seconds respectively. The TIME function will be used to add the hour, minutes or seconds.

Text Functions

Excel has quite a good number of text functions, which are used in order to manipulate a string of texts. The & operator is for instance used in order to join strings.

The LEFT function will be used to extract the characters that appear leftmost from a string.

The RIGHT function will be used to extract the rightmost characters form a string.

The MID function will be used to extract part of a string starting from the middle.

The Len function will be used to get the length of the string

The FIND function will be used in order to find a certain part of a string in a given string.

Use SUBSTTUTE function in order to replace an existing text with another text in a string.

Financial functions

There are financial functions that are very popular in Excel, which are the Pmt function, Rate (for calculating interest rates), Nper, Pv (present value) and Fv (future value)

Lookup and reference

These are the Excel's lookup and reference functions such as HLOOKUP, VLOOKUP, INDEX, MATCH and CHOOSE.

The VLOOKUP function represents the vertical lookup and this is used to look for a value that is at the leftmost column of a table, and then return a value from another column that you specify in the same row.

The HLOOKUP function represents the horizontal lookup. It is used in a similar manner as the vertical lookup function.

The MATCH function will be used to return the position of a value in a given range.

The INDEX function will be used to return a specified value in a two-dimensional range or a one-dimensional range.

Lastly, the CHOOSE function will be used to return a value from a list of values, based on a certain position number.

Statistical functions

Here are some of the statistical functions you will encounter in Excel.

In order to calculate average of a certain range of cells, the AVERAGE function will be used.

The AVERAGEif function will be used to average cells based on a single criteria.

The MEDIAN function will be used to find the median or the middle number.

The MODE function will give you the most frequently used number.

The STEDV function will give you the standard deviation results.

The MIN function will be used to find the minimum value

The MAX function will be used to get the maximum value.

The LARGE function will give you the third largest number while the SMALL function will give you the second smallest number.

Round

To round numbers in Excel, you will use these three functions: ROUND, ROUNDUP and ROUNDDOWN. Remember that if a number is rounded in excel, its precision is lost.

The Round function isused to round a number to two decimal places.

The Roundup function is used to round a number up, away from zero.

The Rounddown function on the other hand is used to round a number down, towards zero.

Chapter 3:
Excel Formulas

An Excel formula is basically an expression which you will use to calculate the value of a given cell. Functions are basically formulas which have been predefined already, and they exist in Excel. Excel formulas will help you make calculations on data that has already been written on the program. The formulas here are always linked to the Excel data; therefore if anything changes on the data, the changes will be reflected easily for you to see. One of the things you will find so useful to use while using formulas in Excel is the fill handle. With this, you will not need to copy one formula over and over again across the worksheet. This will save you a great deal of time.

Formulas in Excel can be used to basically add or even to subtract numbers. There are more complex calculations that you can do with Excel formulas too, for instance making deductions in payrolls, finding an average in a list of numbers, calculating mortgage payments among others. Good thing with Excel is that if a formula is entered correctly and there is a change in the data that has been used in the formula, the program will automatically make the changes and update the answer by default.

To get started with Excel formulas, you need to understand the concepts of absolute referencing. Remember that the data that will be used in Excel formulas does not necessarily have to come from the same worksheet. You might be required to use data in other worksheets on one single formula, which is why it is important to learn how to integrate data in Excel too.

Always start with an equal sign. This is a little different form the actual mathematics because all Excel formulas are supposed to start with an equal sign. Example: =5+8. In this case, the equal sign will go into the cell where you want your answer to appear. The presence of an equal sign is significant in Excel as it informs the program that what follows is part of the formula and not a different value. Once this formula is entered, the cell containing the formula will show the answer and the formula will automatically go to the formula bar.

Entering a formula

To enter a formula in Excel, select a cell where you want the formula to be applied, then let Excel know what you want to get in that cell. If for instance you use an = sign, you will get the sum total of the cells that you will elect. The results will come automatically.

Editing a formula

When you select a certain cell, the formula bar will automatically show you the value or the formula. If you want to edit the formula, just click on the formula bar and make the changes you have in mind. Once the changes have been made, hit Enter.

Use of cell referencing

This will help you to write a formula in such a manner that when the data is changed, the results will change automatically without the need to change the formula. What you do here is to enter your data in the worksheet cells and then informing the application the cells which will be used in the formula. This way, in case there are changes to make, you will only change the affected data in the cells and not the formula. This is done by use of a cell reference, or an address of that cell. In cell referencing, you need to know that cells are made by an intersection of a vertical column and a horizontal column. You start naming a cell from its column, which is identified using alphabets ABCD, then its row which is identified by numbers 1234. A cell reference is therefore a combination of the column letter and the row number. For instance A1, B2, C3 and so on.

The operator precedence

There will always be a default order in Excel in which calculations will be occur. If for instance there is a part of the formula in parenthesis, that is the part that will be calculated first. After that, multiplications and divisions will follow. Once this is done, the program then adds and subtracts as per the remaining part of your formula.

Using =B1*B2+B3 as an example, Excel will first of all deal with the multiplication, that is B1*B2, then it will add the results to B3.

If this was the formula, B1*(B2+B3), then the results will be different because Excel will first of all calculate what is inside the brackets, then multiply the results with B1.

Chapter 4:
Data Analysis

Microsoft Excel is not just a program for storing data but also a program through which youcananalyze and manipulate data for a very long time. Excel has great features which can help its users to analyze data with use, through its Analysis Toolpak. This is an add-in program in Excel, which comes with very powerful data analysis tools that can be used for statistical, financial and engineering data analysis. Here are some of the features you will find in Excel for data analysis:

Sort

This is the feature that you will use in order to classify your data. You can forinstance use this feature to sort your data in just one column or different columns, in a descending or ascending order. In order to sort just one column, select it then on the Data Tab, click on AZ in order to sort it in an ascending order. If you need the data sorted in a descending order, you will instead click on ZA. If on the other hand you want to sort data in a number of columns, start by clicking Sort on the Data tab. A Sort By drop down menu will appear, from where you will select a specification of your choice. Click on Add Label, and then select the columns that need sorting.

Conditional formatting

This is the feature that enables you to highlight some or all of your cells in a certain color. You can do this according to the value of your cells. Choose conditional formatting feature from your Home Tab, the select the kind of formatting you want on the cells you will select.

Filter

This feature will be used only when you want to display those records that meet a certain criteria. In order to do this, click on one of the single cells inside your data set, then select Filter on your Data tab.Make your selections then hit OK.

Tables

Tables are great because they help you to analyze your data in Excel more quickly and very easily. It is therefore important to learn how to insert a table in Excel, how to sort and filter in a table and also how to display a total row at the end of your tables. In order to insert a table, select any single cell in your data set, and then click on Table on the Insert Tab. You will automatically get a nicely formatted table from Excel. Chose the style of a table you would like to work with.

Charts

Creating charts in Excel is very easy and charts can be used to display a lot of information, more than a worksheet full of numbers. To create a chart, select a range where you want to create a chart from, then chose Line on the Inserttab that is in the Charts group. You can select Line with Markers for a better view. Once your chart has been created, you canchange it to a different type of chart with simplicity. You can switch the rows and the columns as well, any time. If you need your chart to carry a certain title, inserting the title will be easy too.

Solver

This is a tool that is included in Excel, which uses different techniques from different operation research in order to get the most favorable solutions for all manner of decision problems you will face. You will have to add this feature to your Excel though, in order to enjoy using it. To do this, select Options form the File Tab, then under Add-ins, choose Solver Add-in, and then click on the Go Button. Once it has been added, hit Ok and you will be able to find your Solver tool on the Data Tab.

The what-if analysis

This is a feature that will allow you to try out different scenarios or values for your formulas. You can use a Scenario Manager to create various scenarios, in order to see how different outcomes will appear from a data set you have already created. This helps a lot in decision making.

Chapter 5:
Macros

Macros in Excel are very important tools. They willgive you a chance to performnumerous operations by a click of just one button,or through changing a cellvalue or even by opening a workbook. Macros are meant top help you work efficiently, smartly and faster. The advantage yougetintheuse of macros is that your workload is reduced by a great percentage, helping you to work more, and accomplishing your tasks faster.

Macro is a very popular program that is present in most ofthe Windows applications. Some of the Windows apps providetheir users with some inbuilt Macro programming to help them work better, for instance the program can be found in MS Excel, in MS Word among other applications. Use of macro is a technique you should learn if you want to enjoy use of Excel.

In MS Excel, you can record or write your own Macros depending on the need you have.

Macro recording

It is important to learn how you can record macro in Excel. To get started, open your Excel workbook, and then choose the Developer Tab of your workbook. Click on the Record Macro button. It is at the right hand side of the Top Menu Bar. Give this Macro a good name. You can also create ashortcut that you will always use in order to run this particular Macro. Select a location too, where you wantyour Macro stored. Once you are done, hit OK.

Do something in Excel sheet, for instance editing some values and then click on the Stop Button as you start running the Macro at the same time. The results will be a recorded code in the given Macro Name.

Running Macro in Excel

There are two ways through which you can run your recorded macro in Excel:

i)   Through pressing the Run Button

ii) Through pressing Alt+F8

When you run the Macro, the changes that were recorded in the Macro will automatically appear on the worksheet.

Macros are supposed to automate tasks in Excel

Use of macros in Excel formulas

Like I mentioned earlier, macros are supposed to make your working with Excel much easier. They allow you to record and store some of the important tasks that you intend to use again, and you can do this with just one click of a button. If you are worried about making errors whenever you are making calculations for instance or you do not want to delay in a certain task, macros are just what you need to work with.

When using macros in Excel formulas, start by opening the Developer Tab in your Excel workbook. This will be found at the Excel options, and once the menu window opens, go to the box next to have Developer Tab showing on the Ribbon. Click Ok

Now change the security of macro in your worksheet in order to allow the program to run. This will be done on the Developer Tab, from where you will get Macro Security. Enable all Macros there, and then hit OK.

Now write the formula that is to be use in the Macro. If it is already written, cut it from wherever it is and paste it there.

Go to the Developer Tab once again in order to enter the Macro information. Choose Record Macro and once the window is open, type the name of the macro in the dialog box and select a storage location for your macro. Go to the Developer Tab, and then click on Record Macro. Right click on the spot where you want your macro to be stored and the click Past from the drop down menu. Now press Stop Recording Macro on the developer Tab and you are done. If there is more information that is needed for the macro, use the description box to add it to the macro and then click OK.

Use of variables in Excel Macros

Variables are ordinary objects in programming which serve as provisional storage locations for data. They help a lot especially for people who want to use macros to make their work easier and faster because they allow for flexibility in the use of macro designs.

To use variables in Excel macros, start by declaring the variable you want to use and its data type. Excel supports up to 17 types of data including integer, long, variant, string, Boolean, currency among others.

After the declaration assign a data value to that variable. You can do this using the equal sign, which is the assignment operator or through a function call.

Now use the variable just the way it is need in order to process the macro.

Chapter 6:
Ms Excel 2016

Ms Excel 2016 is the program that is in the MS Office 2016 Suite. This is a program of great help to anyone in need of a program that will help them organize and calculate data in Excel 2016.

Ms Excel 2016 comes with all the features and functionalities that you are used to as well as some additional features and enhancements which makes working with excel easier, effective and more productive. There are so many new features you should get to use but only if you upgrade to the latest MS Excel program.

Here are some of the best features you will get once you upgrade to MS Excel 2016:

1. **_Key database improvements_**

    This is one of the things that you will find very useful in the new MS Excel 2016. The database developments include an addition to some of the previous programs that were added to the previous Excel programs. For instance Power Query and Power Pivot are great additions that make the upgrade a great idea to go for. In the new program, you will be faced with options to choose from when it comesto use of data models, reports, pivot tables, power queries, one click forecasting among others. These should help you in the creation of interactive control panels and reports.

2. *Power maps/3D*

These aremapping tools that have been added not just in MS Excel 2016 but also in some of the previous newer versions. These are very helpful because they canhelpyou compareyour data much easier than before, for instance such data as temperatures, population in a given area over a certain period of time and so on. You get to have your images presented in 3D, which is clearer and easy to interpret. This is a great feature touse because you can always record data, then watch as it changes with time and space. This will make it easy for you to come up with a story that can be shared and understood easily by other people.

3. *New charts in Ms Excel 2016*

You get up to 6 new charts that will help you to present your data accurately an easily to your clients and colleagues. Creating such charts has been made much easier. This can be achieved through the database table, from where you select Insert, then Recommended Charts, from where you will be required to choose the kind of chart you feel is right from the data type you want to present. Have a look at the pictured samples in order to make the right choice of a chart to create.

4. *Great quick analysis tools*

The quick analysis tools are supposed to help you save time and energy and they do this by helping you work faster and follow the right route with your data. With MS Excel 2016, things are much better and easier. Once you are done with data entry, select the entire data and click on the icon that will appear at the right corner of the range. That should give you a drop down menu with so many options on what you can do with your data. Click on what you want to do with your data and you will get more options that should direct you to where you want to go.

5. *Ink equations*

This is a new feature that will change your handwritten equations to text, so that they will be easy to transfer to your documents. You can use anything you want in order to write the equations on mathematical problems, which will then be converted to text

6. *New templates*

MS Excel 2016 has new templates which comes with sample data and also charts which are meant to guide you on how to use the templates. You get to benefit from free hand-on exercises as well, so that you can master the skill perfectly before you start using the templates. This helps you to avoid expected errors on the first days of using Excel templates. You do not have to start afresh on your own template; try to add some new data to the sample data spreadsheet provided and it will automatically change based on what you have added into it. Replacing Excels sample data with your real data saves you a lot of time. Excel will do the rest for you, depending on the template that you will choose to use.

7. *The smart lookup*

This is just the same as having internet so close that you can use it for whatever you need as you work on your data in Excel. With this feature, you have great sources of information for instance Wikipedia, Oxford Dictionary, Bing among others. To use this feature, right click on any word or phrase and then select the Smart Lookup option from the drop down menu. You will get accurate information pertaining to the subject on one side and imageson the other side.

8. *Easy association and sharing*

It is now very easy to get other people involved in every data that you create in MS Excel, thanks to the new collaboration and sharing feature in MS Excel 2016. You are now able to share great ideas with other people, data, reports, queries among others. You can also work as a team on charts, worksheets, pivot tables, databases among others. If you want to share, there is a share button at the top right corner, from where you will save the data that you want to share with others.

Chapter 7:
Excel Shortcuts

Using excel does not have to be boring; it can be veryeasy and exciting as well, but only if you use some of the shortcuts mentioned here in your day to dayworking with Excel. So many people are using MS Excel every day. Marketers for instance need it the most especially when creating reports that need to be presented in a meeting or even to analyze data. Creating a report in Excel is not easy; it can be time consuming and tiring. Everyone keeps wondering if there is a waythey can enjoy creating such reports and saving time at the same time. This iswhere Excel shortcuts come in. There are so many shortcuts that you canuse in Excel in order to make your working much easier and to enable you to accomplish your tasks much faster:

Shortcuts that will help you navigate between workbooks, worksheets, through rows and columns include:

1. Shift+ Enter- will help you move through a selection

2. CTRL + ↑- **will help you to jump quickly to the top of a column**

3. CTRL + ↓- **will help you to jump quickly to the bottom of the column**

4. CTRL+. -To jump quickly to the corner of a selection. You can repeat this in order to rotate to each corner on your worksheet

5. CTRL + D in order to fill a cell that has been selected with the content that is the cell above the one that has been selected.

6. CTRL + Shift + F6 in order to switch to the previous workbook window

7. CTRL + w- in order to close an active workbook window

8. CTRL + Shift + Tab to switch to the previous open worksheet

9. CTRL + Tab to switch to the next worksheet that is open.

10. F11 to start a new chart sheet

11. CTRL + r to fill a cell that is selected with content that is in a cell that is to the left of the selected cell

12. Shift + F11 in order to insert a new worksheet

13. CTRL + y to repeat your last action

Shortcuts that will help you with your formatting

Formatting is one of the toughest things you will have to do in Excel especially if you are not sure about what needs to be done. These few shortcuts should help you to format easily and faster:

i) CTRL + F will help you to replace values

ii) CTRL +Shift +% will show all your values in percentages

iii) CTRL + Shift + $ will change all your values to currencies

iv) CTRL + Shift + &will be used in order to apply an outline boarder to the selected cells.

v) CTRL + Shift + : will be used to insert the current time

vi) CTRL + Shift +) will be used to unhide selected columns

vii) CTRL + Shift +~will show all your values in the general format of numbering

viii) CTRL + 3 + i will be used to remove italic formatting in the selected cells

ix) CTRL + Shift + (will be used to unhide selected rows

x) CTRL + 2 in order to remove or to apply a bold formatting to the selected cells.

xi) CTRL + 9 will be used to hide rows

xii) CTRK + 0 will be used to hide selected columns

xiii) CTRL + ; will be used to insert a date

xiv) CTRL + k will be used to insert a hyperlink

Excel Formula Shortcuts

Formulas are the hardest bit to work with in Excel. They are very important though and everyone who finds Excel useful will have to use formulas all the time. Here are some shortcuts that will make your formula use easy and fast:

- Use the = sign in order to start a formula
- Use Alt + Shift + t in order to insert an auto sum formula
- Use F2 or CTRL + u in order to edit a cell that is active
- Use CTRL + a in order to display the formula builder once you type in a valid function name in a formula

Shortcuts to be used to select rows and columns

It is a good thing you do not have to manually drag and select columns and rows in Excel, because this can be very tiring and time consuming. Here are some shortcuts that can help you with this:

a) Shift + ↑ or Shift + ↓ will help you to expand your selection by one cell upwards or downwards respectively.

b) CTRL + Shift + Arrow key will expand your selection to the last cell that is not empty

c) CTRL + Spacebar will select the entire column

d) Alt + ; will select only the cells that are visible in the current selection

e) Shift + Spacebar will select the entire row

f) CTRL + a will select an entire worksheet

Conclusion

MS Excel is one of the most important programs that is in use in many offices today. It is a spreadsheet program that will allow you to make a list of items and store it up in data form and also to categorize information across different sheets within an Excel document that is referred to as the workbook.

There is a lot that beginners need to learn about Excel to be able to use it for data storage and analysis. First of all, uncover the story behind the numbers because there is no spreadsheet program out there that can help you work with numbers better than MS Excel. This program makes it easy for you to work with numbers. Learn how to store, format and edit your data and text in order to keep your workbook organized.

Formulas and functions on the other hand will help you to make calculations as well as to solve mathematical problems, whether small or large. With all the shortcuts you will get to learn in the use of Excel program, you should be able to take full advantage of these feature in order to hack any issue that you face in your workplace or even as an individual that has got to do with numbers.

Another important thing to learn inMS Excel is how to protect yourworkbook using passwords in order to protect your data from manipulation withoutyour consent.

MS Excel skills will make you a more skilled individual than you were, which should open many opportunities for you in this competitive world.

www.ingramcontent.com/pod-product-compliance
Lightning Source LLC
Chambersburg PA
CBHW070522210526
45169CB00027B/1439